CARD FORT

A New Po

Foulsham's New Popular Handbooks

CARD FORTUNE TELLING

A COMPARATIVE STUDY OF THE BEST ANCIENT AND MODERN METHODS BY

C. THORPE

LONDON
W. FOULSHAM & CO LTD
NEW YORK · TORONTO · CAPE TOWN · SYDNEY

W. FOULSHAM & CO LTD
Yeovil Road, Slough, Berks, England

ISBN 0 572 00160-6

Printed in Great Britain by
St Edmundsbury Press, Bury St Edmunds, Suffolk

Contents

Illustrations

Preface

No one knows the origin of Card Fortune Telling, as it is shrouded in mystery. But right back through the ages, the Hebrews, the Chaldeans, the Egyptians, and the Chinese used cards, or tokens, for this purpose. It is only in modern times that cards have been used for games. In this book some of the older, as well as the newer, systems of fortune telling are described.

It will be seen that in some of the systems there is a fairly close resemblance to astrological lore—some of the cards being used, almost as the planets are, as significators. Then, too, the arrangement is also astrological for some of the lay-outs.

This book does not propose to justify card fortune telling; it only sets out what are claimed to be the best methods of divining by means of cards. But, on the other hand, it is suggested that a study of the occult will reveal that there may be much more real depth in the subject than appears on the surface.

Acknowledgement is due for some details derived from Sepharial's compendium of *Fortune Telling by Cards—Cartomancy*, to Professor Foli's *Fortune Telling by Cards*, and to *The Tarot*, by Papus.

History teems with instances of successful cartomancy, or card fortune telling. These are well known, and the interest displayed in attempts to foretell the fate is felt to be sufficiently great to warrant bringing out a volume of this kind, giving examples of the various arrangements and the rules for reading the card.

C. THORPE

1

Introduction

As with nearly all subjects of similar character, there is a diversity of opinion as to the real history of the art of divination by cards. Sepharial, for example, inclines to the belief that it is one of the oldest modes of prediction, and that it has been practised in various ways, from the earliest periods. Both the Chinese and the Egyptians, he asserts, had engraved metal plates or tokens, the former of copper and silver, the latter of gold, which they used for the purpose.

The Egyptian plates, 78 in number, were the work of the great magician, Hermes, and contained symbolical matter and numbers, a page on each, of the great Hermetic book. The division of the book was into two arcanas, the major and the minor. The former contained 22 of the plates, the latter the other 56.

It is said by Sepharial that the Hermetic plates contained, in addition to their symbolic figures, astrological material of immense use in divination. 'The 12 signs of the Zodiac, the 7 Sacred Planets, the 36 Decans, the 360 Degrees, and their corresponding genii, of the Zodiac—these symbols entered into the construction of the hieroglyphs.'

Unfortunately, the complete original key to the mysterious book of Hermes was lost, but some of the lore has been handed down orally, and some partly preserved by secret societies of initiates in all ages. Thus, we have today comparatively modern transcriptions of the more ancient ideas.

Dr Papus, a learned French *litterateur*, has produced the most exhaustive book on the Tarot of the Bohemians. This, he suggests, has been 'transmitted by the Gypsies from generation to generation . . . the primitive book of ancient initiations'. It contains, according to this writer, 'the explanation of the exalted philosophy and science of ancient Egypt'.

Mr A. E. Waite, who writes a preface to the book throws some doubt upon the authenticity of the historical details, but explains the closeness of the parallel between the symbolism of the Tarot and the Hebrew Kabbalah, or Hidden Wisdom. This 'work of Papus,' says Mr Waite, 'will appeal only to serious students, and it will be worth their while to take up his elements and seek to construct them independently'.

Another writer on the subject, Professor Foli, tells us that there is no authentic, or verified history of cards going beyond the last five hundred years, though he himself in another place refers to the 'prevalent belief of their antiquity in other forms'.

Ordinary playing cards, as we now know them, seem certainly to have been derived from the Bohemian Tarot; but these in turn seem to have had an origin which is lost in antiquity.

Foli refers to the Gypsy theory. He carries the tradition back beyond Egyptian days to the early Hindus, and to a migration from them of a low caste through Egypt and so to the West.

Recent studies in anthropology, and symbolism generally, certainly afford some grounds for attributing the use of cards or plates of metal to very ancient times. Nearly all our customs have come down to us from very remote periods. In fact, all our laws are really survivals of customs, the first observance of which is beyond all human power to discover.

Professor Foli says, 'It is certain that at first cards were called by the name *naibi*; and the Hebrew and Arabic words *nabi*, *naba*, *nabad*, signify "to foretell." It is also widely believed that the idea of playing games with cards was an afterthought, and that their original purpose was for the practice of divination'.

Coming now to more recent times, we find several names standing out as popular exponents of cartomancy. Madame Lenormand and Etteilla are two of the most famous. Each of these had a special method of laying-out, which will be described later. It will be seen, however, that the significations of the cards themselves are very similar.

Another method is that of Sepharial, whose works on astrology are very numerous, profound and dependable. Sepharial bases his methods largely on astrological bases. This will also be briefly described later.

Then there is the work of Papus, to which we have already referred. It would be impossible to summarise this, but some details will be given.

2

The general signification of the cards

There is a very general agreement as to the significations of the individual cards, which are, however, modified by the positions in which they occur in relation to each other. As to the symbolism of the pack as a whole, this is evident when a few correspondences are pointed out. There are four suites—these correspond to the four seasons—spring, summer, autumn, and winter, and to the four divisions of the day—morning, noon, evening, and night. They also correspond to youth, manhood, maturity, and old age.

For determining the general ruling of the cards, diamonds may represent youth; clubs, manhood; hearts, maturity; spades, old age.

In the work of Papus, in dealing with the Tarot cards, the four suites of which are sceptres, cups, swords, and pentacles, these are shown to correspond with clubs, hearts, spades, and diamonds. Then four general principles are given. The clubs represent enterprise and glory, the hearts love and happiness, spades hatred and misfortune, and diamonds money and interest, or, more briefly, enterprise, love, hatred, and fortune.

In his book Sepharial details this a little more fully. Diamonds are said to represent life generally, and so are influenced by the other cards. Hearts are generally to denote friendships, sympathy, love attachments, and peace.

Clubs represent power, arising from position, fame, acquirements, or natural accomplishments. Spades, loss and privation—its own meaning is modified if other cards are near to influence the spade. A run of spades by themselves is a very dismal and ominous portent.

When an enquirer desires to consult the cards one of these is allotted to him or her to indicate the enquirer's personality. A man takes a King, a woman a Queen, and the particular suit chosen is governed by the colour characteristics of the consultant.

A very fair man or woman takes the Diamond King or Queen as significator. Persons with very light hair, blue or grey eyes, use Diamonds. But Diamonds are also used to denote those with grey or white hair.

For those of a slightly darker type than the 'Diamond people' Hearts are used—they are still distinctly of the fair class of complexion, but not so fair as Diamond people.

From this it may be inferred that Clubs and Spades are for the fairly dark, and the very dark people respectively. Clubs are brown-haired and brown-eyed people. Spades are black-haired folk with very dark eyes, quite black or very nearly approaching it.

A point to which attention must be directed here is that a reversed card has its meaning modified. In some packs it is fairly easy, by noting the difference in the top margins, to detect a reversed card. But generally speaking now that card printing is so regular, it is better to ensure the detection by marking the cards at one end by a pin prick or a little dot.

Usually only thirty-two cards are used for fortune telling—the two's, threes, fours, fives and sixes being thrown out. In one method that will be detailed thirty-six cards are used—the four twos are added. The Tarot pack consists of seventy-eight cards, but in some of the delineations only a part of these are used.

Generally the meanings of the cards remain fairly constant for all the methods. Thus a good-omened card is always such—but the particular or specific meaning of it is altered somewhat by the method of using it. For example, the Ten of Spades by one method means 'losses,' and, if reversed, 'tears'; in another, 'grief,' and, if reversed, 'passing trouble.' The Seven of Spades may mean 'hope,' and, if reversed, 'friendship'; or it may be 'resolve,' and, if reversed, 'difficulty in love affairs'.

Here, then, we give in sequence a general table of card values that will give the normal indications of the cards. Starting therefore with the order first given, we take Hearts and Diamonds, then Clubs and Spades.

HEART VALUES

Ace: Good news, a house, a love letter; *reversed,* disappointment, removal, or a friendly visit

King: Kind-hearted, loving man of fair complexion; *reversed,* an uncertain, inconstant lover

Queen: A generous loving woman, fair; *reversed,* crossed in love and capricious

Jack: A pleasure-loving bachelor, a friend or lover; *reversed,* a lover with a grievance

Ten: Good fortune and happiness; *reversed,* changes, a birth

Nine: Success, the wish card; *reversed,* passing troubles

Eight: Love, invitations, thoughts of marriage; *reversed,* unreciprocated affection, jealousy

Seven: Contentment and favours; *reversed,* boredom and jealousy

DIAMOND VALUES

Ace: Marriage offer, ring, bank notes; *reversed,* demand for debt, bad news

King: Fair or grey-haired man, widower; *reversed,* treachery and deceit

Queen: Fair woman, widow, a gossip; *reversed,* untrustworthy, a flirt

Jack: An official, a messenger; *reversed,* mischief-maker

Ten: Journey or removal, finance; *reversed,* misfortune

Nine: Anxiety, news; *reversed,* danger, family quarrels

Eight: Amorous, short journey; *reversed,* affections ignored

Seven: Child, unfriendly criticism; *reversed,* scandal, minor successes

CLUB VALUES

Ace: Good luck, papers or letters bringing in money, or good news; *reversed,* ill news, delayed letter

King: A dark man, friendly and straight; *reversed,* worries and slight troubles

Queen: Dark woman, affectionate; *reversed,* undependable, perplexities

Jack: Athlete, clever, good lover; *reversed,* luck may change

Ten: Ease and prosperity, journey, luck; *reversed,* sea voyage, estrangement

Nine: Legacy; *reversed,* obstacles

Eight: The love of a dark man or woman, joy and good luck in consequence; *reversed,* documents causing trouble, litigation

Seven: Success with money; *reversed,* financial worries and losses

SPADE VALUES

Ace: Satisfaction in love, high building; *reversed,* sorrow, death, disappointments

King: Widower, untrustworthy lawyer; *reversed,* a very dangerous enemy, impending evil

Queen: Widow, faithful friend; *reversed,* intrigue, treacherous woman

Jack: Doctor or barrister, bad mannered; *reversed,* deceitful, traitor

Ten: Long journey, grief; *reversed,* slight sickness

Nine: Failure, financial or domestic; *reversed,* death of dear friend

Eight: Impending illness, sorrow; *reversed,* rejected affection, evil living, quarrels

Seven: A change for the worse, a resolution; *reversed,* accidents or losses

These meanings, or values, of the cards should be well studied and committed to memory, so that when any particular card appears a key to its interpretation is at once presented to the mind of the reader. The word key is used advisedly, because the terms or values are not to be taken as the absolute determination of the cards, but rather as a guide to the specific values in relation.

If there is a run in any particular suit, it will be seen that Clubs will be an omen of the very brightest character, while a similar run of Spades will indicate the worst possible phases of fortune. A run of Hearts will foretell successes in love, of Diamonds in money.

Combinations of Court cards are important. Amongst others the following may be noted:

When the Aces come together, they denote new surroundings. How this will affect the future fortune depends upon the influence of the cards that follow them.

Sepharial suggests that the Aces coming together always portend a change of life. Foli thinks they imply danger and financial loss. But this is lessened if they are reversed; three Aces, temporary trouble. Kings coming all together denote business, or, as another authority has it, 'honours, preferment, good appointments'. If reversed, of less value, but arriving earlier. Three Kings are a good omen unless reversed, Four Queens imply talk and scandal, or a social gathering spoilt if the cards are reversed. Three Queens denote friendly visits, but, if reversed, possible danger to the consultant. When the Knaves come together, workmen or agents about the house, or roistering and noisy conviviality. Three betoken annoyances from friends. If reversed, the evil is not considerable.

Four tens or four nines stand respectively for good fortune or surprises. Three tens are very bad, but three nines good. Four eights, a mixed omen of success and failure. Three eights, new family ties. Four sevens, trouble is imminent; three, ill-health, loss of friends.

3

Some simple, but effective tellings

THE PAST, PRESENT, AND FUTURE

The pack of thirty-two cards must be well shuffled by the enquirer and cut with the left hand into two heaps, which can be as equal or unequal in size as the enquirer fancies.

After the cut, the two heaps must not be placed together again until the top card of each has been laid aside, face downwards, to form the usual Surprise. The remaining cards are then squared up and dealt into three heaps of ten cards, which represent respectively the Past (left-hand heap), the Present (centre), and the Future (right-hand heap).

The ten cards of the first heap—the Past—should be spread in a row from left to right and then examined for pairs, triplets, and quadruplets, according to our Table of Meanings. You should carefully note all reversed cards as they tend to lessen the good predicted, or increase the evil, as the case may be. Such cards usually refer to opportunities lost. It is also very helpful to notice which suit predominates in each heap, Clubs being the most fortunate and Spades the most evil. This predominance of colour shows whether the greater amount of success has been reached by the enquirer or is still to come.

After this the cards should be read singly, by their several meanings, from right to left of the row.

When all these have been thrown aside, the centre heap, representing the Present, is similarly examined and then the Future.

Finally, the Surprise is consulted to see what unexpected event is going to influence the life and fortunes of the enquirer.

THE FOUR ACES

This is a very simple method for determining a single question or wish. The thirty-two cards are well shuffled by the enquirer—the Diviner then deals off thirteen cards, face upwards, on to the table, and makes a careful search for the four Aces. If any are found, place them, face up, by themselves. The remainder of the pack, including what are left of the thirteen, are then re-shuffled as before, and the Diviner again deals out thirteen cards and searches for further Aces.

This can be done for a third time, but that is all. The earlier the four Aces appear, the better it will be for the enquirer—if in the first deal, it is exceptionally fortunate; if in the second, it is certainly very good luck—as a rule, they are not completed till the third attempt has been made.

Those that appear in each deal should be kept separate, as it is very important to notice the order in which the suits appear. This will clearly show the amount of effort needed before the wish or question is satisfactorily answered—for instance, if the Spade Ace appears first of all, the enquirer must be prepared to face trouble and difficulty, even should all four Aces appear in the course of the first deal.

This is a very useful method to know, as several questions can be dealt with in a very short time, and there is no need to remember any list of meanings. It is as well to limit the questions to three, however, as the cards are never so reliable when overworked, or tired.

Another simple method for answering a single question is worked with the full pack of fifty-two cards. First remove the type card representing the enquirer, King or Queen, as it happens to be. Then have the fifty-one cards well shuffled and cut into three heaps of any size. They should be cut towards the right by the left hand—the enquirer makes the first cut, placing the upper portion of the pack on the right and then cuts this latter heap into two.

The Diviner takes the centre heap (originally the middle of the pack) face down in his hand, adds to it the right-hand heap (originally the top of the pack), and finally the left-hand heap goes on top of all. Now make a circle of forty-two cards, face down, on the table—inside this make a triangle of the remaining nine cards.

The enquirer must now turn over any fifteen cards, replacing them, face upwards, in the original positions. When this is done, read them according to the number of each suit exposed.

THE SEVEN ANSWERS

The thirty-two cards are to be shuffled and cut once, as usual with the left hand, and the enquirer should wish once during this process.

Then the cards are dealt out, one by one, so as to form seven heaps—six of these to form a semi-circle—the cards for these being placed face downwards while the seventh heap is built in the centre and the cards are dealt face upwards.

The seven packs represent 'yourself' (*i.e.*, the enquirer); 'your home'; 'what you expect'; 'what you don't expect'; 'the Surprise'; 'what is sure to come true'; and 'your wish'.

It will at once be noticed that some heaps will contain five cards each, others only four each. The heaps should be arranged from left to right—the first card dealt starting the heap on the extreme left and the seventh card going, face upwards, in the centre.

Some Diviners employ this method but only use seventeen cards—the pack is shuffled and cut as before, but only the first seventeen cards are dealt. This method is certainly simpler, as the heaps only contain two or three cards each; it is also thought to be a great advantage, as the exposed cards naturally vary greatly as regards the proportion from each suit. If you use the full pack, there must of necessity be eight of each suit; whereas if only seventeen are dealt, six or seven or even eight of one suit might appear on the table, and it is obvious that the preponderance of any suit would greatly affect the reading.

Some Diviners object to the seven packs, maintaining that it is false art to have one heap for 'what you don't expect,' and another for 'the Surprise'. The sixth heap is also rather feeble, and certainly looks as if it had originally been included to make the number uneven. This School of Diviners therefore deal off thirteen cards only from the full pack of thirty-two, and build up only five heaps for 'yourself'; 'your home'; 'what you expect'; 'the Surprise'; and 'your wish'.

A WEEK'S HAPPENINGS

The enquirer should well shuffle the pack and cut them with the left hand into three heaps, as before explained.

The Diviner now takes the top card of each heap face downwards, and places them so as to start a row of fifteen cards, the top card of the left-hand heap being first removed. The cards are then re-shuffled and cut as before, the Diviner again removing the top card from each heap and adding them to the row. This is repeated five times, so that fifteen cards, face downwards, are ranged on the table from left to right.

The Diviner now turns over, face upwards, the extreme card at either end and reads the meaning which applies to the following day—special importance attaches to the suit colours which will certainly show whether that day will be a fortunate one or not.

In many cases the inner meaning of the cards is never considered at all, this method being used on the Continent to determine, simply and solely, which will be the fortunate and unfortunate days in the week—Sunday counting as the first day, of course. Remember that the right-hand card is the more important —for instance, a Spade on the right and a Club on the left would indicate that things would certainly go wrong in the early part of the day, but would rapidly improve after noon. Whereas a Club on the right and a Spade on the left would indicate a prosperous morning, followed by a calamitous afternoon and evening.

When using this simple form of Divination, no list of meanings has to be consulted, which in many cases is a great advantage; it is therefore an excellent companion method to the one already described for answering questions by the suit colours of the cards turned up.

Fourteen cards are turned up in this way, two and two, leaving the centre card face downwards on the table. The Diviner should now note, on a slip of paper, the point values of each pair of cards, in case the enquirer should be confronted on that day by any business or other matter in which figures are concerned. For instance, if a Nine of Spades and a Seven of Hearts are the cards for the following Tuesday (the third day), then anything involving nine or any multiple of nine should be avoided, and those things involving seven should be followed up. Suppose anyone calls and whishes to make an appointment, fix the seventh, fourteenth, twenty-first, or twenty-eighth day of the month. Should the *seventh day* (*i.e.*, the next Tuesday) fall on the ninth, eighteenth, or twenty-seventh of the month. it would obviously be a bad day to select. In the same way, if the fourteenth, twenty-first, or twenty-eighth of the month was the ninth day following, that also would prove a bad day.

With all these particulars to help him, or her, along, your client should be able to avoid all mishaps and make the best use of the opportunities for good fortune that might come his, or her, way.

The fifteenth card is used to answer one question, which, in this case, must be a spoken one. The suit of the card determines whether the answer is to be 'yes'; 'probably'; 'doubtful'; or 'no'— and the pip value should be noted if it can be made to fit in any way, as that particular number will have a fateful influence, one way or another, over the matter in question. Its influence, however, only lasts for the week in question, so if it is a Spade, it is wise to warn your client to delay and wait for a more propitious time before proceeding with the matter in his mind.

THREE QUESTIONS ANSWERED

This is a simple method of Divination that does not require any consultation of Tables of Meanings. The pack of thirty-two cards must be well shuffled by the enquirer and cut into three unequal heaps, using the left hand. That portion of the pack that was previously in the centre is now placed at the bottom; the top section is placed above this; and the original bottom section is placed on top.

The cards are now spread out fanwise on the table, face downwards, taking care that every card is visible and that none overlap and hide a neighbouring card. The enquirer must now think of a question, and while doing so should choose three cards and place them, face downwards, on the table.

He, or she, should now think of the second question, and while doing so pick out seven cards, placing them separately on the table, also face downwards. While the third question is being thought of, thirteen cards must be chosen and the remainder of the pack discarded.

The Diviner now turns up the first heap of three cards and determines from these the answer to the question—in this method the lower the value of the cards the less the opposition to the success of the enquirer, the more fortunate the result of his enquiry. The suit colours must also be considered as affecting the result, but the greater importance rests upon the value of the cards—in this case the Ace, of course, is counted as the lowest and most fortunate card in the pack.

Similarly the second heap of seven cards, and the third heap of thirteen will be turned up, each in its turn, and the answer considered.

This is not only a simple but a quick method of Divination, but obviously it only applies to answers to definite questions.

DIVINATION BY OBSTACLES

Have a pack of thirty-two cards well shuffled and cut once only. Pick out the type card representing the enquirer and hold the rest of the pack face downwards in your hand. The type card is placed in the centre of the table, the top card from the pack is turned over and placed above the type card, the second card being similarly placed below. The third is now placed on the left and the fourth card on the right. The fifth card is placed upon the type card, covering it. The Diviner now discards eight cards altogether, and, that being done, adds another card to each of the five in the same order as before— above, below, left, right, and upon the type card.

Discard eight more cards and place the final five cards as before, one by one, upon the heaps. Read each heap in turn, beginning with the one from above the type card, and only looking out for pairs and triplets, suit colour, and whether the four high cards (the Ace here being counted with the Court cards, as this method is older than the one last described) or the four low cards predominate—the latter being the personal effort of the enquirer, and the Court cards being the help or interference of other people.

DIVINATION BY PAIRS AND TRIPLETS

This method is not so old as some of the others but is very pretty and effective, besides being reliable.

The pack of thirty-two cards must be well shuffled and cut into three with the left hand, these being arranged as before explained, taking the original centre section for the bottom of the newly arranged pack. The prepared cards are now held in the left hand and the three top cards are turned up. If they contain two or three cards of the same face-value or three cards of the same suit, they should be placed face upwards on the table—the others being discarded.

This is repeated till the pack is exhausted, the odd two cards being discarded.

The discarded heap is now well shuffled and cut three times as before—this must always be done by the enquirer and never by the Diviner, who merely deals or arranges the cards and gives their meanings as they appeal to him. Diviners who are slightly clairvoyant make some marvellously accurate predictions without apparently studying the accepted meanings of the cards.

The cards having been shuffled the second time, leaving the selected pairs and triplets face upwards on the table, they are again gone through in sets of three as before in order to increase the row of fateful cards on the table, any odd cards at the end being discarded as at first.

This process is repeated for a third time before the final fateful row of cards is consulted. You can now give a general opinion upon the prospects before the enquirer by a study of the prevailing suits and by noting whether Court cards or plain cards predominate, or you can go further and pick up the cards, two at a time, taking one from each end as in previous methods. This can always be done when cards are arranged in a row, by whatever process they have been selected—always bearing in mind that the right-hand card is more active and positive than the left-hand one.

A very quick, though perhaps rough and ready, method of Divination is to let the enquirer choose thirteen cards haphazard after the pack has been well shuffled and cut once. As chosen, they are placed face upwards across the table from left to right, and the answer to the question is decided by the predominant suits and by the number of Court or plain cards thus selected. Should there be an equal number of cards belonging to two or more suits (obviously with thirteen cards there cannot be an equal number of Court or plain cards), you give preference to that suit that has most cards on the right of the row—these being more active and aggressive.

DIVINATION BY THE SPADE SUIT

The pack must be shuffled and cut into three heaps and rebuilt, as before explained.

The Diviner now holds the pack face upwards in his hand—this is different from most methods of Divination, where the the cards are generally dealt from the top of the pack. Each card is looked at, but unless it is a Spade, it is placed on the table, face upwards, to form a fresh pack. As soon as a Spade is reached, that card is also discarded, but the next following card is placed, face upwards, on the table to start the necessary fateful row of cards. Should two or more Spades come together, only the first one is discarded, the other or others being added to the fateful row in front of you, together with the next card following the last of that batch of Spades.

This is continued till the pack is exhausted, when the discarded heap is taken up and treated in the same fashion *without being re-shuffled.*

This process is repeated for a third time, and then the type card must be looked for—if it is not already in the row, it must be found and added at the end. The Diviner now counts the third, seventh, and thirteenth card from the type card, in each case counting the type card as one. These three cards are not removed from the row, but can be pulled down a little below the level of the others, as they form the dominant trio in this method.

This counting is done to the left, and when you reach the extreme card, the one first put on the table, you go back to the end card at the right and so continue your count if necessary. But it often happens that all three dominant cards are reached before you come to the card on the extreme left. Of these three cards, the one finally nearest the right is the most powerful. It clearly depends upon the position in the row of the type card itself whether the third seventh, or thirteenth is the important card.

It is generally agreed that by this method only near events can be predicted, certainly it does not cover more than a month.

A somewhat similar method is used in England with the full pack, but instead of using the Spade suit as the guide for the cards to be picked out, you go by the points of the cards—the Ace in this method counts as one. The pack having been shuffled and cut into three heaps and rebuilt as before, you deal the cards from the top, placing each one face upwards on the table as you do so. While you do this, you count aloud: one, two, three, four, five, six, seven, eight, nine, ten, Jack, Queen, King, one, etc.

If any card, irrespective of suit, turns up at the proper count—for instance, if the fifth card really is a Five, it is placed as one of the fateful row, and the counting continues as before.

When the pack is exhausted, the discarded cards are turned over and dealt out again as before, turning each one up in the Spade suit method; but you must be careful after the second time to note at which card you cease calling, as when you start the third deal you do not restart the counting at one, but continue from where you left off.

In addition to the cards that turn up at their own proper calls, you also add to the fateful row any cards that turn up three or more at a time, whether at their proper call or not. Thus three Tens, three Fives, would be added, merely because they follow each other in value, but three Hearts or three Spades would be ignored, as in this method the dealing takes no account of suits.

The Diviner now forms a rough cross from the cards in the row, placing the first card from the extreme left to form the top of the cross; the next card to form the bottom of the cross; the third to form the right, and the fourth the left wings. The next four cards are built above these in the same way—top, bottom, right, left, and so you build the cross till all the chosen cards are used up.

The top heap is read first, as the predictions from those cards are supposed to come first; then the bottom heap; then the right and then the left—the latter, of course, being very far into the future. You can allow roughly a fortnight for each heap.

THE DECISION BY ACES

The pack of thirty-two cards must be well shuffled and cut into three and rebuilt. The Diviner now turns up three cards at a time—if an Ace appears among them, or the type card representing the enquirer, or the Wish card (Nine of Hearts), those three cards must be taken out and placed face upwards on the table. This continues till the six cards are all exposed, *i.e.*, the four Aces, type card, and the Wish card. Those sets of three cards not containing one or more of the six fateful cards are to be discarded altogether.

When the necessary cards are obtained, they must be gathered together, re-shuffled and cut, and dealt out once more in sets of three, retaining those sets only that contain one or more of the six cards of Fate. This is repeated for a third time—if the six cards are now gathered together within a total of nine cards (or fewer) the Wish will prove successful. If in twelve, the result is doubtful; but if over twelve, the reply is negative. If under nine, then the fewer the cards, the quicker and more decisive the result.

The following is the record of an actual test and will show how it works: The type card was the King of Clubs, as a dark man was the enquirer. The first three cards turned up were the King of Diamonds, Ace of Spades, and King of Clubs—these were retained on the table, as they included both an Ace and the type card. The second set were the King of Spades, Queen of Spades, and Ten of Diamonds—these were discarded as useless. The third set were the Ten of Hearts, the Six of Diamonds, and the King of Hearts, and were also discarded. The fourth set were the Seven of Spades, the Eight of Spades, and the Ace of Diamonds, and were kept. The fifth set contained the Nine of Diamonds, Eight of Clubs, and Ace of Clubs, and of course were retained. The sixth set were the Jack of Clubs, Ten of Spades, and Ace of Hearts, and were left on the table; while the seventh set completed the first deal, as it contained the Jack of Spades, Nine of Hearts, and Five of Clubs.

The remainder of the pack, therefore, was added to the discarded heap, and the fifteen cards, face upwards, on the table, were gathered together, well shuffled, and again dealt in sets of three, with the following result; First came the Ace of Spades, Nine of Hearts, and Jack of Spades; then the Ten of Spades, Ace of Hearts, and Nine of Diamonds. These were followed by the King of Diamonds, Five of Clubs, and Jack of Clubs, and of course, these three cards were at once discarded to the satisfaction of the enquirer. Then came a set consisting of the Seven of Spades, Ace of Diamonds, and Eight of Clubs, which were retained; and, finally, the Eight of Spades, Ace of Clubs, and the King of Clubs, which were also kept.

These twelve cards were now gathered and shuffled for the third and fateful deal, the result of which was as follows: The first set contained the Ace of Hearts, Nine of Hearts, and the King of Clubs—a very good start, giving us three of the necessary cards at once. The second set contained the Nine of Diamonds, Jack of Spades, and Eight of Clubs, indicating some obstacle or difficulty to be faced, as none of these cards were of any use and clearly delayed the gratification of the enquirer's wish. Then came the Ace of Clubs, Ace of Spades, and Ten of Spades, thus destroying all hope of immediate success—but the final set commenced with the Ace of Diamonds, thus enabling us to get out at the tenth card. This is quite good, and shows success after some small delay or difficulty—indeed, it is always reckoned satisfactory if the six fateful cards can be secured at the eleventh. Six or seven would show startling and unexpected good fortune; eight or nine is extremely fortunate; ten or eleven quite satisfactory; twelve or thirteen are very doubtful; while fourteen or fifteen may be looked upon as a distinct negative.

There is another way of deciding a question by the Aces which is a general favourite and is considered very reliable.

The pack, being well shuffled, is cut once only with the left hand. Thirteen cards are then dealt from the top, face upwards, and if any Aces are among them, they (the Aces only) are retained. The pack is now re-shuffled and cut, and again thirteen cards are dealt and any Aces are removed. This is repeated a third time, and if, in these three deals, the four Aces have all been secured, the enquirer may feel satisfied that his wish will be granted.

Should the Aces be secured in the second deal, or in the first (a very rare occurrence), the result naturally will be very much more favourable. But if in the three deals only three Aces are secured, the result is doubtful—whereas if fewer than three turn up, the wish will not be gratified.

There is still another method of working by the Aces—it is rather more elaborate and a favourable result is not so easily obtained. First of all pick out the four Aces, the type card to represent the enquirer, the Nine of Spades to represent disappointment, and a seventh card to represent the question itself—if about money, this would be the Ten of Diamonds; if about business, then the Ten of Clubs; if about a woman, then the Queen nearest to her in suit colour; if about a man, then the corresponding King. For any general wish, choose the Jack of the enquirer's own suit to represent his thoughts.

These seven cards are shuffled but not cut, and are then spread, face downwards, in a row on the table. The remainder of the cards are then well shuffled and cut once and are turned up in a row on the table, seven at a time. The object is to find the Wish card, represented by the Nine of Hearts. Should this card appear in the row of seven, count its position from the left and turn over the corresponding card in the row of fateful cards lying, face downwards, on the table. Should the Nine of Hearts not appear in the first seven cards repeat the process as before till you come to it.

If the card thus reversed is the Nine of Spades, that settles the enquiry at once by an emphatic negative—if not, the whole performance is repeated and a second card reversed in the fateful row of seven. If the fateful Nine of Spades is once more avoided, the process is repeated for a third time—the appearance of the Disappointment card after the second deal is not, of course, so emphatic as if it is reversed at once, but it is still a negative, though with no attendant disaster or unpleasantness. If it is discovered after the third deal, there is still a chance of success if the enquirer is keen enough to take the necessary trouble over the matter.

The methods given so far are all well-known and in universal use, but in the present chapter we have given some very effective methods of Telling, which at the same time are perfectly simple. We wish to draw special attention to the fact that four of these methods can be used at once by the student, as no List of Meanings has to be learnt or studied—these four methods are 'The Four Aces'; 'A Week's Happenings'; 'Three Questions Answered'; and 'Decision by Aces'.

4

Star methods of laying-out

One of the most general methods of laying-out the cards is called the Grand Star, of which we give a diagram on page 33. For this purpose the thrity-two cards of the short fortune-telling pack are used—the Deuces, Threes, Fours, Fives and Sixes are discarded.

A card to represent the enquirer or consultant is selected. If he is a fair man, the King of Hearts is chosen as the card to represent the enquirer. This card is called the significator. If a very fair man or a white-haired man, the card for significator is the King of Diamonds. These two suits are used also for very fair or fair women, the Queen being the significator.

Clubs and Spades represent respectively consultants who are between dark and fair, and very dark persons. Kings and Queens are used for the two sexes. If the enquirer is a widower or widow, Spades is the suit for the significator.

The diagram should now be consulted, in order that the correct mode of laying-out the cards can be seen. First of all the significator is placed on the space numbered 1, and the other cards, in the manner now to be described, placed in proper order upon their correct positions.

After shuffling, first by the operator and then by the consultant, the cards should be cut with the left hand by the consultant.

When the first cut has been made, ten cards are dealt, and the eleventh is taken as the first of the lay-out and placed on the space numbered 2 in the diagram. All the remaining cards, thirty in all, are now treated as a pack, cut again by the consultant, and the top card is placed on space No. 3.

Again the cards are treated as a pack, again cut, and the bottom card of the cut placed on No. 4. This is repeated constantly, taking a card alternately from the top of the bottom half of the cut pack, and from the bottom of the top half of the pack until sufficient cards have been withdrawn to make up the completed Grand Star.

When, after cutting, the pack is re-made, the top part, which has been cut, should be placed at the bottom of the pack to make it ready for the next cut.

For reading the fortune the cards are taken in pairs. Beginning with the outside row of pairs, moving from left to right, contrary clockwise, thus, 14 and 16; 21 and 19; 15 and 17; 20 and 18. The inner circle is next taken in pairs, moving in the opposite direction, from right to left, as a clock's hands go. Thus, 10 and 6; 12 and 9; 11 and 7; 13 and 8. The four centre cards are read in pairs, thus, 4 and 2; 5 and 3; and the last card, 22, is taken individually. All the cards are read, of course, in special relation to the position each bears to the significator.

Generally, the modifications arising from position are as follows: cards that are directly above the significator show the possibilities of success and achievement. Those directly below denote that which has transpired. To the right of the significator the cards denote that to which the enquirer is approaching, his wishes coming to fulfilment. Those to the left mark obstacles and opposition to be feared.

In addition to these direct positions, there are those that are right and left above, and right and left below, when regarded obliquely. Those to the right above should show helpful signs, to the right below things accomplished toward the desires of the enquirer. To the left above there will appear the obstacles that may arise out of past conditions to thwart the desires, and the left below those that have already made themselves apparent in the past.

When reading for the Grand Star, some general indications may be gained from groups. Thus, if three or four Kings, Queens, Knaves, or Aces are shown, these will give a general idea that must be taken into consideration in reading the pairs.

As an example of Grand Star reading, Foli gives the following:

THE GRAND STAR

'The consultant is represented by the King of Hearts, a fair open-headed, good-natured man, and the pairs come out as follows: Queen of Diamonds and King of Spades (14 and 16); Knave of Hearts and Ace of Diamonds (21 and 19).

'Nine of Clubs (reversed) and Queen of Clubs (15 and 17) Knave of Spades and Eight of Diamonds (reversed), (20 and 18), Ace of Spades and Queen of Spades (6 and 10); Knave of Diamonds and King of Clubs (9 and 12); Queen of Hearts and Eight of Clubs (8 and 13).

'Nine of Diamonds (reversed) and Knave of Clubs (7 and 11); Ace of Hearts and Ten of Spades (4 and 2); Nine of Spades and Ten of Hearts (5 and 3); the Ace of Clubs is 22.

'Here the consultant is connected with (14) the Queen of Diamonds, a fair woman with a tendency to flirtation; she is amusing herself with (16) a very dark man, probably a lawyer, of ambitious and not too scrupulous character who does not wish well to the enquirer.

'The next pair shows the Knave of Hearts, representing Cupid, or the thoughts of the one concerned, linked with (19) Ace of Diamonds, a wedding ring. While this important item is occupying his thoughts he gives a small present, the Nine of Clubs, reversed, to (17) Queen of Clubs, a charming dark lady, who is the real object of his affections.

'The Knave of Spades (20), figuring a legal agent, or the wily lawyer's thoughts, makes mischief, and (18) Eight of Diamonds (reversed) causes the enquirer's love-making to be unsuccessful. (6) Ace of Spades warns him against false friends who will frustrate his matrimonial projects, and in 10 we find one of them, the Queen of Spades, a widow, with possible designs upon him herself.

'The Knave of Diamonds (reversed) (9) shows the mischief-maker trying to breed strife with the enquirer's trusty friend (12) King of Clubs, and (8) Queen of Hearts, a fair, lovable woman possessing (13) Eight of Clubs, a dark person's affections. (7) Nine of Diamonds (reversed) tells of a love quarrel owing to (11) Knave of Clubs (reversed) a harmless flirt.

'The enquirer will get (4) the Ace of Hearts, a love letter, but his happiness will be succeeded by (2) Ten of Spades, a card of bad import. (5) The Nine of Spades, tells of grief or sickness, possibly news of a death. But (3) Ten of Hearts, counteracts the evil and promises happiness to the enquirer, who shall triumph over the obstacles in his path and find (22) joy in love in life.'

It will be seen here that cards of evil import are made of little avail by their association with those of better omen, and the general indications from the groups is here quite fair.

THE SIMPLE STAR

Another method of using The Star—see diagram page 36—is with fifteen cards in all. To tell the fortune in this method, place the significator first of all on the centre position marked C (consultant).

Shuffle the cards as previously directed, and let the consultant cut the pack into three. The cards thus cut are to be turned up and used as the basis for the drawing for the star. From the centre portion of the pack take the first card thus exposed and place it upon 1. From the left-hand portion of the pack take the top card for 2. From the right-hand portion of the pack the card for 3. The fourth card is taken from the centre portion, and so on until twelve have been drawn.

To determine the thirteenth and fourteenth cards, re-make the pack, and let the consultant shuffle and cut. Then take the top card of the bottom half for the fourteenth. These should be placed directly above the significator, as shown in the diagram.

These two cards are very important indications, and must be read finally as denoting what is likely very soon to come to pass. The general meanings of the cards may be used for the reading, with the modifications resulting from the positions as they come out.

Another method (recommended by Minetta), is called 'The Week'. First obtain the significator and place this in the centre. Then shuffle the thirty-one remaining cards. Let them be cut by

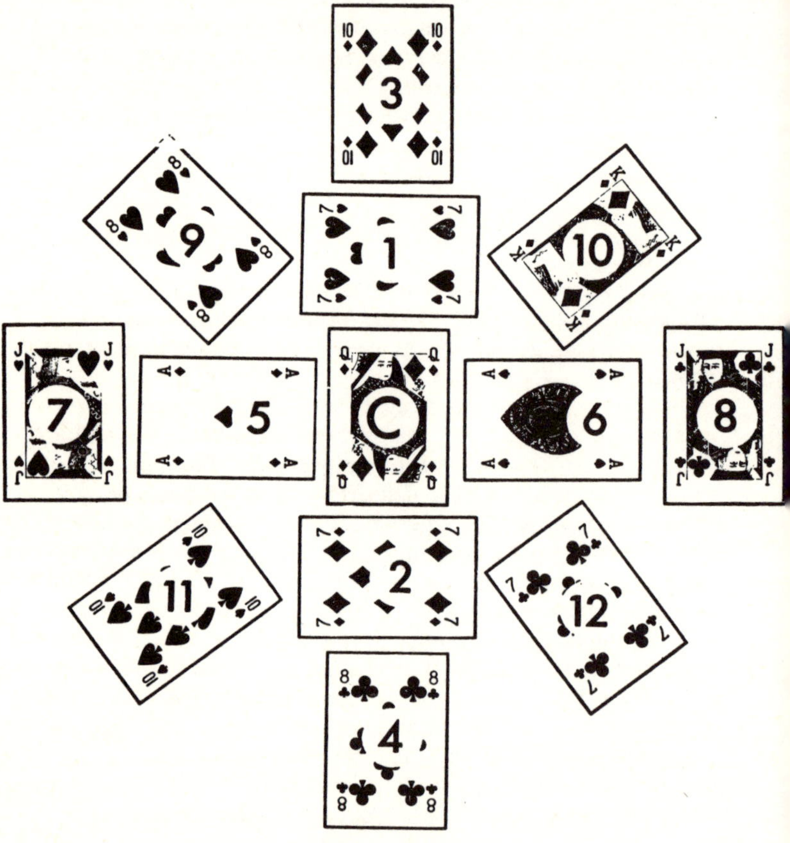

THE STAR

the consultant. Seven cards are then taken in order from the cut, the first being that on the top of the bottom pack.

These seven cards are arranged in a semi-circle over the consultant's card, beginning at the left. Each card must then be covered by another. The covering cards, without their faces being seen, may be placed upon those below in any order. The cards are then read in pairs from the left.

An example is given by Sepharial. The first pair were Seven of Spades and Ten of Hearts. This indicates a removal from town. The next were the Ten of Clubs and Eight of Diamonds—a short journey. Next, Seven of Diamonds and Nine of Spades—illness of child or a pet.

Next came Ace of Diamonds and King of Clubs—a letter from a dark man. Next, Eight of Hearts and Nine of Clubs—an invitation to festivities. Next came the Ten of Diamonds and Ace of Clubs—a letter with money; and finally the King and Queen of Hearts—the visit of a married couple.

Taken altogether, this is seen to be pretty good. There are only two Spades in the lay-out, and one of these is almost nullified in its evil influence by being in association with a Heart. Without the Heart it might have meant a change or removal, and, with evil influences, danger or sickness, for example.

In an ordinary lay-out, if the King of Clubs, representing the consultant, were to appear between the Ace of Diamonds and a Ten of Hearts, the omen is particularly fortunate. It would indicate that the enquirer is on the eve of a very happy marriage. On the contrary should the cards on either side be the Nine of Spades and the Ace of Spades reversed very evil results may be looked for. The enquirer is in danger of death, or at least of serious illness.

THE STAR OF FIFTEEN

Take the pack of thirty-two cards and select the type card, placing it face upwards in the centre of the table. The enquirer must now well shuffle the pack and cut it once only with the left hand. Take the pack and spread it out fan-wise and let the enquirer choose fifteen cards, one by one, placing them one by one, and face downwards, in a heap by themselves. Discard the remaining cards and pick up the chosen fifteen, holding them face upwards.

Place the first card to the left of the type card, representing the enquirer; the second card to the right; the third card goes above, and the fourth card below, thus forming a simple cross. The fifth card is now placed upon the type card itself.

Repeat this process with five more cards, thus increasing the size of your cross—and again with the final five cards. The type card will now have three cards on each of the four sides; while the fifth, tenth, and fifteenth cards will have been placed upon the type card itself, covering it.

Now take each set of three cards by itself and read their meaning according to the table, being specially careful to watch for reversed cards as well as for pairs and triplets. Also carefully note if two or more of the three cards are of any one suit, as that greatly affects the result.

The set of three cards on the left should be read first of all, as they represent the immediate past of the enquirer; then the set of three on the right which govern the immediate future.

After these, if it is wished, you can read the three cards of the upper set, which show the more remote past and which, consequently, are somewhat affected by your reading of the left-hand set. Balancing one set carefully against the other you should be easily able to decide if things are improving for your enquirer—or if they are drifting for the reverse.

Now consider the bottom set of three cards, which refer to the more remote future, and, after reading their meaning, noting reverses, pairs, triplets, and suits as before, you must balance these against the right-hand set and thus determine which way the future will tend. Suppose, for instance, that apart from their individual meanings, there are two Spades in the right-hand set and either one or no Spade in the bottom set, then the enquirer may certainly look forward cheerfully to a lessening of any difficulties that may be facing him at the moment.

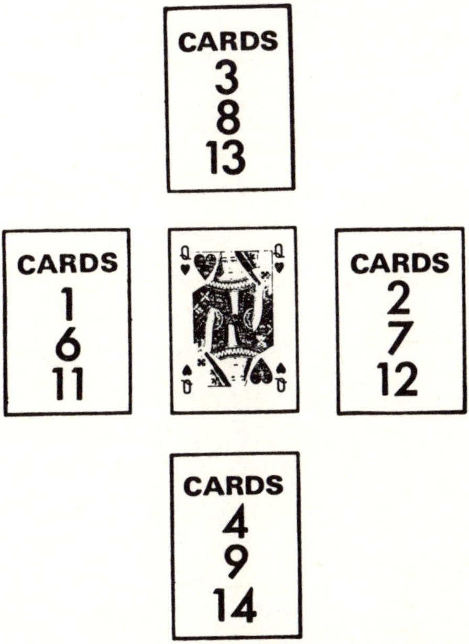

CARDS 5, 10 AND 15 ARE PLACED UPON THE CENTRE CARD OF THE STAR

THE STAR OF FIFTEEN

The central set of three, covering the type card, gives your answer to any special wish or question of the enquirer's—they do not apply to the past or future and therefore need not be read as regards their individual meanings. Go by the suit colours, making any necessary allowance for the presence of two or three cards of the same value.

5

Methods of great Diviners

Two of the best known exponents of card fortune telling were the famous Madame Lenormand and the no less famous French master, Etteilla, or, to use his real name, Alliette.

Lenormand's method employs 36 cards—the four deuces or twos are added to the usual pack, and the cards are laid out, in four rows of nine each, as shown in the diagram on page 43.

Sepharial says, 'The cards touching the significator of the consultant must be regarded, i.e. those that are above below, right and left of it, and those that touch it obliquely to the right and left, above and below.

'These nine cards (including the significator), taken in relation to the positions they occupy, will determine the condition of the consultant, his hopes, success, obstacles and dangers'.

All the other cards are read independently, that is, one by one, but having regard to their general significance as a whole. The four deuces are used as follows: the Heart represents the consultant, the Diamond the confidant of the enquirer, the Club an adviser of the enquirer, and the Spade is shown by the position it occupies.

Some general indications may be given in relation to the cards, which are laid out one by one in order, after a shuffle, finally, by the consultant, who then cuts them. Hearts are lucky cards—they indicate love, happiness and good fortune. Although they may be laid upon a position of misfortune or evil import, they help to turn it to good.

Clubs come next in point of good luck. They may be seen principally to indicate friendship of a reliable character Diamonds, on the other hand, seem to denote obstacles, rivalry and jealousy even. Spades are almost invariably the omen of misfortune and disaster.

The cards may be drawn twice—the first time to learn what events lie in the near future, the second time to know those more distant. In each case the operation is identical, remembering always to shuffle and cut before each deal.

THE THIRTY-SIX POSITIONS

1. PROJECT

Hearts: Success in undertakings, when a Heart card falls in this position. The cards accompanying, viz., in positions 2, 10, 36, will show the particulars of success.

Clubs: A faithful friend will work to bring about success for you.

Diamonds: Difficulties caused by jealousy or spite. Note accompanying cards.

Spades: Treachery and serious delay.

2. SATISFACTION

Hearts: Your wish will be accomplished. Many favours await you.

Clubs: Fidelity will surmount all difficulties and give you joy.

Diamonds: You have difficulties to overcome by reason of much jealousy.

Spades: Treachery will diminish your hopes of happiness.

3. SUCCESS

Hearts: Happy and favourable prospects surround you.

Clubs: By means of friends you will gain your desire and have success in your projects.

Diamonds: Many difficulties owing to jealousy and distrust. Nevertheless you will succeed according to your merits.

Spades: Deceit and treachery. There is little hope of success herein.

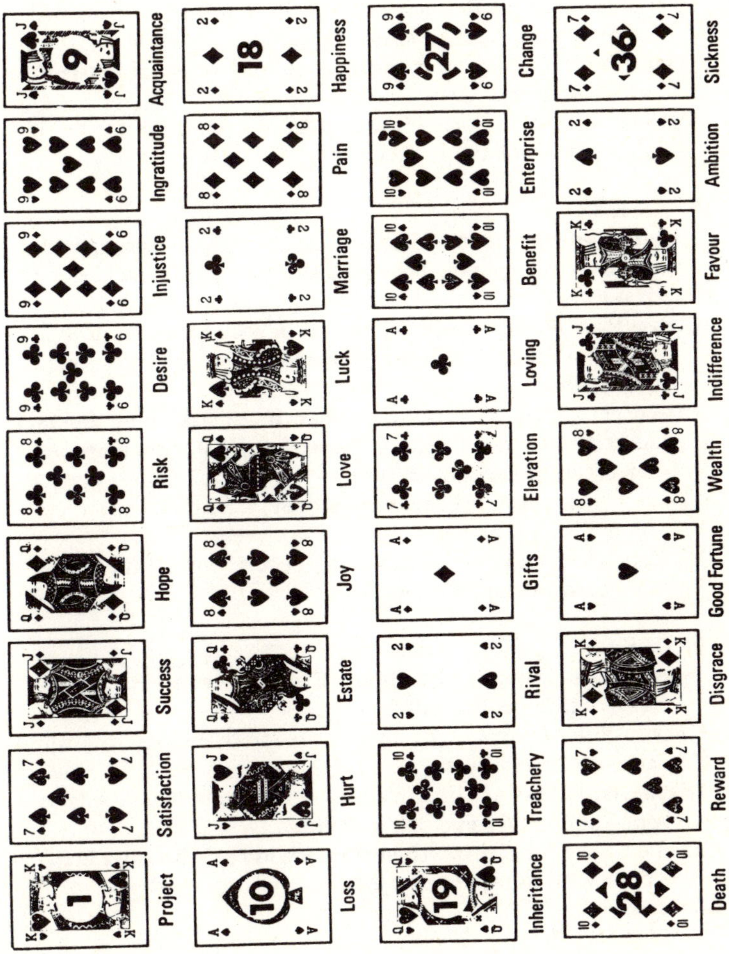
Project
Satisfaction
Success
Hope
Risk
Desire
Injustice
Ingratitude
Acquaintance
Loss
Hurt
Estate
Joy
Love
Luck
Marriage
Pain
Happiness
Inheritance
Treachery
Rival
Gifts
Elevation
Loving
Benefit
Enterprise
Change
Death
Reward
Disgrace
Good Fortune
Wealth
Indifference
Favour
Ambition
Sickness

4. HOPE

Hearts: You will gain your wish.

Clubs: You have good chances of gaining your wish, but you will have to work hard towards it.

Diamonds: Hopes lightly founded or entirely vain will not meet with fulfilment.

Spades: A foolish hope inspires you. Be prepared to see it destroyed root and branch.

5. RISK

Hearts: You will enhance your fortunes by means of unexpected gain. Whatever you have at stake will yield you a good result.

Clubs: You will be benefited and put in the way of securing a better condition than you now are in. You will succeed fairly well.

Diamonds: Expect unlooked-for things. If you ask about money at stake you will get it. In respects your surroundings are uncertain. Look at the cards touching this number. If Hearts or Clubs, good; if Diamonds, money; if Spades, expect loss by fire, water, or other unlooked-for event.

Spades: Very bad risks. Unfortunate speculations, thefts, losses, and even bankruptcy.

6. DESIRE

Hearts: You will gain the object of your most ardent desire. Your wishes will be fulfilled.

Clubs: With effort and by the assistance of others you will accomplish your wish.

Diamonds: Others are interested as well as you. There will be contention and some risk of failure.

Spades: Alter your wish. 'All hopes abandon ye who enter here'. Your wish cannot be granted.

7. INJUSTICE

Hearts: An injustice has been done you, but you will have full reparation and your rights will be recognised.

Clubs: Employ an intermediate. You have every hope that your merits will be regarded.

Diamonds: Make overtures in the shape of presents and gifts. Nothing stands in your way except a feeling of annoyance.

Spades: Forget your wrongs and do not augment them by affording fresh opportunity for injustice to be done to you.

8. INGRATITUDE

Hearts: You will be pleased to receive proof that those who have been ungrateful are anxious to make amends.

Clubs: Your friends will make redress of all slights and ingratitude you have suffered.

Diamonds: Do not be annoyed, jealousy alone is at the root of the ingratitude you have received.

Spades: Do to others as you would have them do to you. Expect disappointment and treachery, but see that you do not offend in this respect yourself.

9. ACQUAINTANCE

Hearts: Your associations will be profitable to you. Certain friendships will be of great advantage to you.

Clubs: You have the best of friends. See that you do not neglect them.

Diamonds: Beware of being a cause of jealousy and strife among your associates.

Spades: Exercise the greatest caution in selecting your friends, but do not be surprised if you are betrayed. You may be of use to others, but will get little from your associates.

10. LOSS

Hearts: Be prepared for the loss of benefactors and those of good heart towards you.

Clubs: Your affairs will receive a rude shock by the loss of a friend.

Diamonds: Guard your possessions and interests, for there is danger of severe losses at hand.

Spades: Deceit and treachery surround you in business. Grief and trouble through losses await you. Beware of false investments, frauds, and thefts.

11. HURT

Hearts: Your affections will receive a hurt which will give you much pain.

Clubs: Friendships will give you sorrow and trouble. Expect the loss of a friend.

Diamonds: Your interests and business affairs will cause trouble. Spite is directed against you.

Spades: Much sorrow is at hand. Be prepared for grief, losses, and treachery.

12. ESTATE

Hearts: You are going forward towards success from day to day.

Clubs: By means of work and good friends you will progress to your satisfaction and acquire wealth.

Diamonds: With some worry and a good deal of opposition you will have success.

Spades: Your estate is falling away. Redouble your efforts and your care, and be watchful of your interests for some time to come.

13. JOY

Hearts: You will have cause for joy in the direction where your affections are placed.

Clubs: Happiness will come to you through your friends and your efforts.

Diamonds: You will be gladdened by overcoming an obstacle in face of opposition and jealousy.

Spades: You will be glad to have been of use to others. Faithful service to a superior will bring its reward.

14. LOVE

Hearts: You will have success and happiness in your love.

Clubs: You have a faithful lover who will advantage you in many ways.

Diamonds: Jealousy, the green-eyed monster, besets the path of uncertain devotion.

Spades: Your affections will be blighted; but do not despair, you will conquer at last by patience and fidelity.

15. LUCK

Hearts: You will have success in life, and prosperity is now coming to you through legitimate means.

Clubs: By your own mental and moral efforts, as well as the help of good friends, you will have more than enough to live honestly.

Diamonds: There is danger of your fortunes being affected seriously through jealousy and rivalry.

Spades: Hate and deceitful dealing will destroy your chances of immediate success.

16. MARRIAGE

Hearts: You will marry well. One whom you love will reciprocate your affection.

Clubs: Your friends will be the means of bringing about your marriage. It will be a well-assorted match.

Diamonds: Trouble, worry, and vexation follow on marriage. If you are in quest of a dowry rather than a wife you will get it. The consequences you must bear with resignation.

Spades: Treachery and malice are the fruits of marriage in your case. Beware how you choose a partner. The Nine of Spades here means divorce, the Eight means separation.

17. PAIN

Hearts: Your troubles will soon pass away. Live in hope.

Clubs: Effect a reconciliation with your friends as soon as possible.

Diamonds: You are troubled because of sharp words and angry feelings. Dismiss them and live in peace.

Spades: You are the victim of deceit and treachery. Bide your time and do not take active measures yet.

18. HAPPINESS

Hearts: Your affections are well placed and reciprocated. Nothing hinders your happiness.

Clubs: With prudence and attention you will touch the springs of happiness.

Diamonds: You seize pleasure with too desperate a hand. You run great risks and are liable to excite anger and jealousy.

Spades: Your pleasures will be of short duration. Be careful they are not the cause of your undoing.

19. INHERITANCE

Hearts: You have every reason to expect a considerable inheritance.

Clubs: You may expect a legacy from a friend.

Diamonds: You will engage in strife and legal proceedings which will cost you more than you gain by legacy.

Spades: If you have any right to an inheritance there is great danger of your losing it by means of deceit on the part of others. Look well ahead, and provide for contingencies.

20. TREACHERY

Hearts: Rest assured that the evil directed against you by false friends and traitors will fall on them alone.

Clubs: You will have time to thank your friends for a timely deliverance from plots directed against your welfare.

Diamonds: Time will efface the effects of treacherous plots and spiteful actions. But you will be very much upset by discovering the danger you are in.

Spades: Scandal, loss of friends, and deceitful dealing are to be expected.

21. RIVALS

Hearts: You overcome all rivalry. The day is yours. Make the most of it.

Clubs: Your own merits and the good offices of friends will secure you a victory over your rivals.

Diamonds: Through some spite and intrigue you may hope for a decision in your favour. The omens are fickle.

Spades: You cannot hope for success in this direction. Your rivals will secure all the favours you expect.

22. GIFTS

Hearts: You will have gifts far exceeding your expectations.

Clubs: Gifts will be made to you for your own sake. Favours from friends.

Diamonds: Be careful of being drawn away from the path of honour by gifts of money and other inducements.

Spades: Beware of any gifts made to you. Treachery and deceit are hidden under smiles and overtures of friendship.

23. LOVING

Hearts: You will be satisfied in the love bestowed on you. You have the affections of a person of good character.

Clubs: You have one of good birth in whom to repose your affections. You will receive benefits from your friends and confidants.

Diamonds: Be careful. Your lover is susceptible to jealous feelings. Beware of strife among your friends.

Spades: You will have cause to regret having placed your affections in a certain quarter. The person is vindictive and deceitful. Your friends are hypocritical and false to a degree.

24. ELEVATION

Hearts: You will rise far above your expectations, and become the object of regard and honour among worthy people.

Clubs: By the fulfilment of your duty you will obtain elevation and competent fortune. Do not neglect your friends.

Diamonds: Rivalry and contention will for a long time defer your advancement.

Spades: Treachery and malice will obstruct your upward path. You are advised to serve and not to strive for mastery.

25. BENEFIT

Hearts: You will receive all the reward you merit, and many benefits from your superiors.

Clubs: You will gain benefits through your friends, to whom you will owe a great deal.

Diamonds: You will only gain part of the benefits you merit owing to contentions and jealousy.

Spades: The benefits you merit will go to another because of misrepresentation and falsehood.

26. ENTERPRISE

Hearts: Your undertakings will meet with success, and you will make your mark.

Clubs: Your ventures will be lucrative, and your friends will be of much use to you in your undertakings.

Diamonds: There is too much competition and rivalry in your field of enterprise. You are liable to be outdone.

Spades: Many of your enterprises will turn to your disadvantage. You will need to look after your affairs with great care and caution.

27. CHANGE

Hearts: You will have a happy and advantageous change in your fortunes. Luck attends you.

Clubs: You will have to thank a friend for a change in your condition which will be of much good to you.

Diamonds: Be careful lest you are thrown out of the frying-pan into the fire. Avoid strife.

Spades: You are in great danger of losing your present position. You have secret enemies to contend against.

28. DEATH

Hearts: Through a death you will gain something you do not expect.

Clubs: A friend will benefit you by a legacy.

Diamonds: You will soon hear of the death of an enemy.

Spades: Your worst enemy is near to death. Your worst days are coming to an end.

29. REWARD

Hearts: You will gain the reward of your labours, and your fidelity will be requited with abundant esteem.

Clubs: You will receive the reward of your work. By means of your friends you will gain all for which you have striven.

Diamonds: Your recompense will be diminished or retarded by jealousy.

Spades: You are in danger of losing by deceit that which is promised or expected.

30. DISGRACE

Hearts: You will soon forget whatever little disgrace you may incur. It will turn to your advantage.

Clubs: A friend is in danger of disgrace. You will resent it. It will pass away.

Diamonds: You will suffer from calumny and spite. Be careful your name is not brought into just reproach.

Spades: You have misplaced your confidence, and in consequence will suffer loss of honour. You will be betrayed.

31. GOOD FORTUNE

Hearts: An unexpected stroke of luck will render your condition a very agreeable one.

Clubs: You will receive a considerable increase in your fortune by the aid of friends and supporters.

Diamonds: Jealousy and the ambition of false friends will be to your advantage.

Spades: In case of pressing need you will receive the assistance of friends. You will be in great danger, even to the life, but you will be providentially potected.

32. WEALTH

Hearts: You will make a brilliant fortune, quite equal to your highest ambitions.

Clubs: Your work and intelligence, aided by the services of friends, will secure you a fortune of some extent.

Diamonds: Persons of an avaricious and jealous nature in whom you have placed confidence will make their fortunes at your expense, or will profit greatly from your own fortune.

Spades: Your energies and talents are doomed to enrich others only. Be therefore discreet in the use of your energies, and try to preserve your rights.

33. INDIFFERENCE

Hearts: You will be indifferent to the future of others, and will thereby lose some of the happiness of life.

Clubs: Your indifference in the choice of friends will often cause you grave anxieties.

Diamonds: Others will gather the fruits you neglect through your indifference to your own interests.

Spades: Neglect of duties and general apathy will cause the loss of money, honour, friends, and health.

34. FAVOUR

Hearts: You will have the favour of wealthy persons, who will advance your interests very much. You are fortunate in gaining affection and esteem.

Clubs: By your sagacity and fidelity you will gain many friends and will receive many favours from them.

Diamonds: You will have difficulty in obtaining any very substantial favours. You have many rivals.

Spades: You had better depend upon your own labours and the fruits of your work, for little or no preferment will accrue to you.

35. AMBITION

Hearts: Pursue your ambitions with steadfastness and you will reap your reward.

Clubs: You will accomplish your ambitions by means of your friends, who will take an interest in your schemes and projects.

Diamonds: The jealousy of relatives and friends will cause many of your ambitions to fall short of attainment.

Spades: You will suffer a serious disappointment in your chief ambition through the treachery and malice of false friends and secret enemies.

36. SICKNESS

Hearts: Your illness will be of short duration. It will be nothing.

Clubs: You have nothing to fear. Your illness will not be dangerous.

Diamonds: Sharp but short illness will prostrate you for a while.

Spades: You will not suffer alone. Your enemies are also afflicted with sickness. But beware of a long trial and have patience.

Note. Hearts show good fortune wherever they fall, and promise success. Clubs show assistance from friends and well-directed personal effort. Diamonds are fickle and show spite, envy, and jealousy. Spades indicate failure, treachery, malice and lack of initiative.

When good cards surround the number under consideration, it gives an augury of the best results; but if Spades or Diamonds fall thereon, and are surrounded by good cards, it promises obstacles and delay. When Spades fall thereon, and are surrounded by evil cards, such as Jacks, Spades and Diamonds, it portends failure in that particular indicated by the number.

The following numbers deserve special comment:

No. 5 equally shows all risk by lottery, cards, or other games, racing, things burnt or flooded, and speculations of all sorts.

No. 6 denotes all and every object of desire, whether money, love, legacy, or anything not as yet attained and not depending on one's own efforts, as do the ambitions No. 35.

No. 7 shows equally the result of all lawsuits, adjudications, the recompense of superiors, etc.

No. 9 includes all associations, such as marriage, partnership, friends, and business engagements.

No. 16. If the consultant is married or under age, then the interpretation is capable of modification.

No. 21. This includes all kinds of rival interests, whether in marriage, love, business, or competition.

Etteilla's Temple of Fortune is fairly easy to lay out, and has the advantage that it preserves the general values of the cards given in the second chapter of this book, on pages 14 and 15.

All the thirty-two cards are used for Etteilla's method. They are shuffled finally and cut by the consultant, and laid out in the order shown in diagram on page 55.

It will be seen that some of the earliest cards to be dealt, the first six, with others, are those which indicate the Past; the next six indicate, with others, the Future; and the last cards to be dealt, with those adjoining them, represent the Present.

A further division is suggested. The inner circle indicates and refers more particularly to the inner life of the consultant, whilst the outer cards represent more specifically his material, worldly, or external affairs.

What has been said before about the necessity of reading the cards as a whole, as well as individually, applies particularly to the Temple of Fortune.

There are very many other systems of card reading. The French have a distinctive method, the Italians another. Differing systems prevail, too, in Spain and Arabia. The gypsies, also, do not follow quite closely any of those indicated here or above.

No useful purpose would be served, however, in this book in detailing all these other methods. It would only lead to confusion. It is far better really to master one, or at most two, different systems, than to dabble in half a dozen, only to meet with a want of success in any of them.

One system must be given a prominent place here because it is that of a well-known and successful occultist, Sepharial. Moreover, it follows very closely on astrological lines, and Sepharial is possibly one of the best modern astrologers, deserving also to rank with the great masters of old in this science.

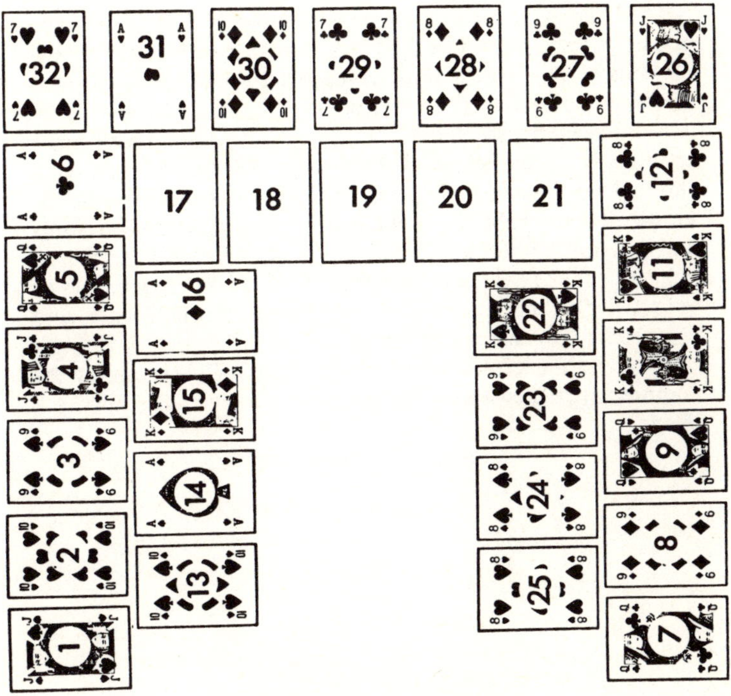

THE TEMPLE OF FORTUNE

A diagram is given on page 57 of Sepharial's system. The twelve celestial signs or houses are used to indicate the positions of the cards, and also to aid in their interpretation. Two cards are laid in each house. One complete round is made first of all, and then the 13th, 14th, 15th, 16th and 17th cards are placed in the centre, as shown.

Then the remaining cards up to 29 are placed around the houses to form pairs, 18 with 1 and 19 with 2, and so on; for the 12 houses. This leaves three cards over, which show in what direction the balance of the fortune lies.

The twelve houses should be learnt first of all. These relate severally (1) to the person of the enquirer, his health and mental state; (2) his financial prospects; (3) letters and journeys; (4) the house, domestic affairs; (5) children, pleasures, etc.; (6) servants and physical comforts; (7) marriage state and what hinders or helps it; (8) financial circumstances of wife; (9) long journeys or voyages; (10) the occupation, the mother; (11) friends and associates; (12) enemies or losses.

Cards in the centre show what immediately surrounds the enquirer, and they should be read both individually and as a whole.

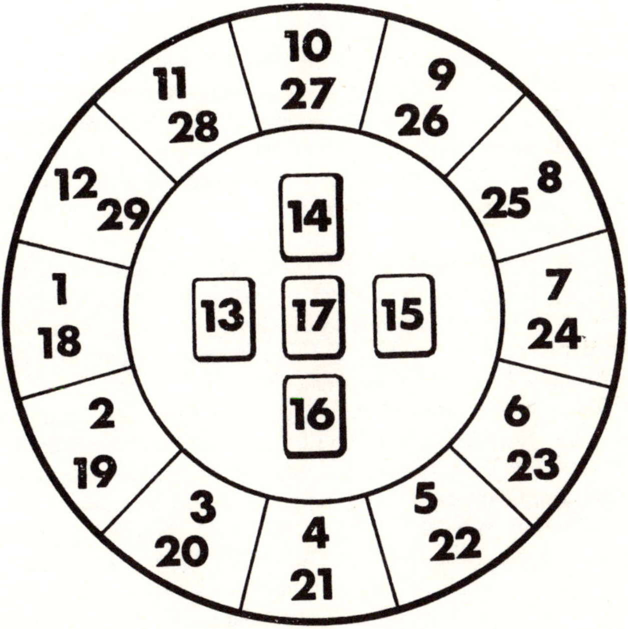

SEPHARIAL'S METHOD

6

The mystic Tarot

As was said earlier in the book, the Tarot was undoubtedly the basis of our present set of playing cards. A brief description of the Tarot set of cards may, therefore, not be out of place. Some of our readers may, perhaps, be inclined to try the more ambitious methods of divination to which the Tarot lends itself, if they see how wonderful it is and how manifold its significances.

There are 78 cards in the Tarot, 22 of which are called the major arcana, and 56 of which are called the minor arcana. The minor arcana corresponds more closely to our present pack of cards. The fifty-six cards which are comprised in it are arranged in four suits, or series, of fourteen cards.

Each of these suits of the minor arcana has four Court cards, and ten plain cards from one to ten. The four Court cards are respectively King, Queen, Knight, and Knave. The Ace does not rank as a Court card, being regarded simply as a unit.

The four suits are called respectively Wands or Sceptres, corresponding to our Clubs; Cups or Goblets, corresponding to our Hearts; swords, corresponding to our Spades; and Money or Pentacles, corresponding to our Diamonds. Here, then, we see why Clubs are considered a favourable omen if they represent power and authority; why Spades are bad, since they betoken swords; why Hearts are good and happy omens, since they represent the cheering or loving-cup; and why Diamonds are emblems of financial success, since in the Mystic Tarot they correspond with money.

The four picture cards, or Court cards, of the Tarot are used symbolically, to represent the Sacred Name, thus:

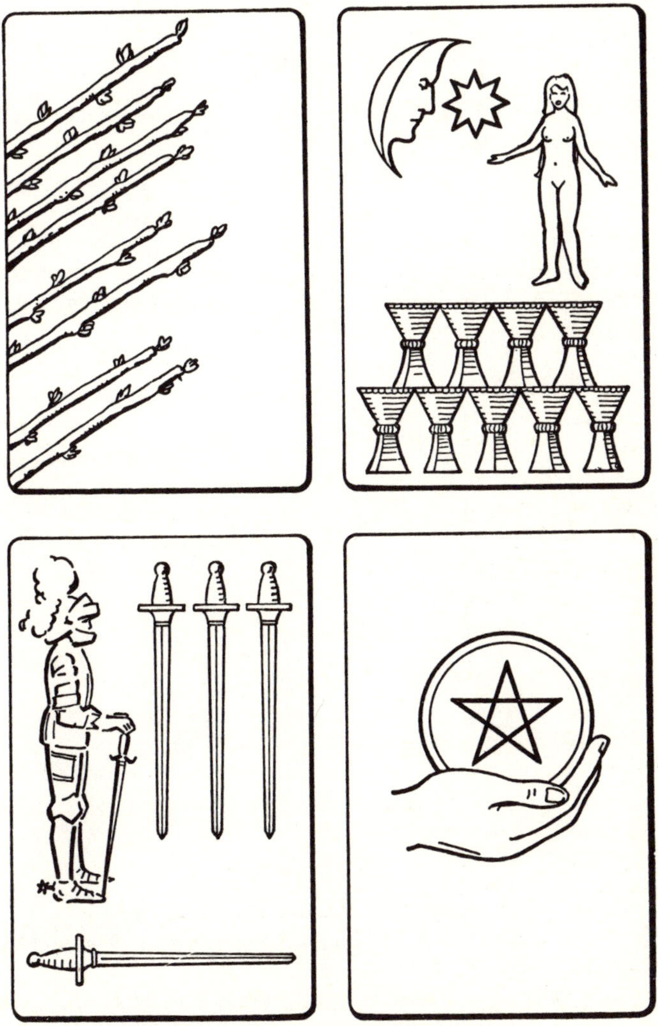

TAROT OR DIVINATION CARDS

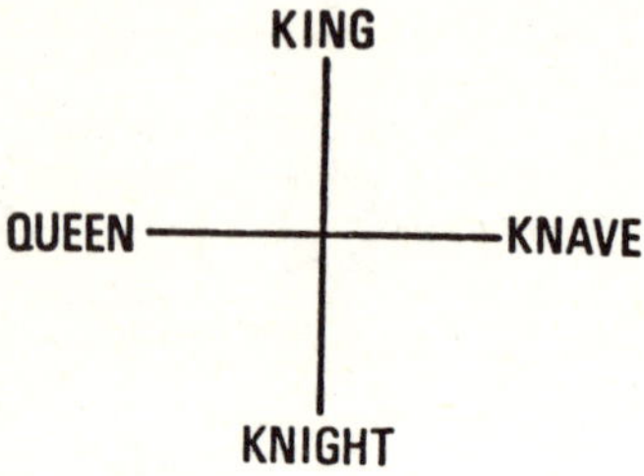

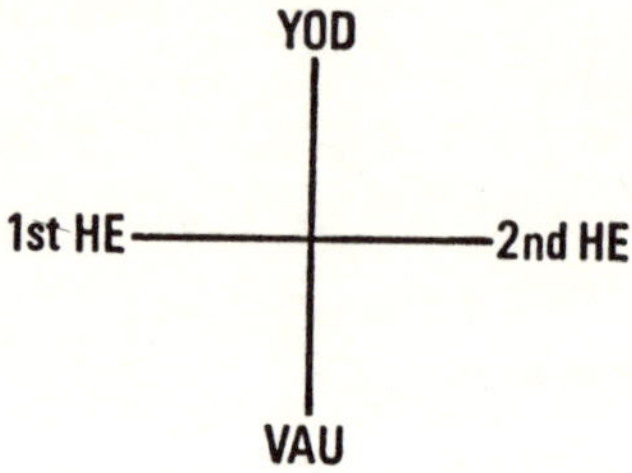

or J.H.V.H.—Jehovah.

Similarly the ten numbers of the suits are arranged as follows:

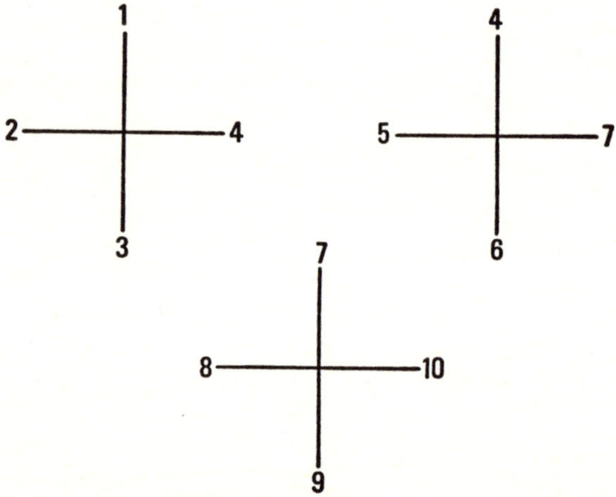

Thus there arises the form that the King is the Yod of 1, 4, 7; Queen is the He of 2, 5, 8; Knight is the Vau of 3, 6, 9; and the Knave is the second He of 10.

These figures are applied mystically in the Kabbalah. The series 1, 2, 3, 4 represent the Divine world; 4, 5, 6, 7, the human world; and 7, 8, 9, 10, the material world.

Further analogies give certain religious affinities with mystical relations on important points. Some writers on the Tarot have paid little attention to the minor arcana, confining themselves almost entirely to the major one. Dr Papus thinks that the minor arcana gives the key to the whole system.

Of the major arcana, the cards are respectively the Juggler or Bateleur (1), the Female Pope or High Priestess (2), the Empress (3), the Emperor (4), the Hierophant or Pope (5), the Lovers (6), the Chariot (7), Themis or Justice (8), the Hermit (9), the Wheel of Fortune (10).

Fortitude (11), the Hanged Man (12), Death (13), Temperance (14), the Devil (15), the Lightning Struck Tower, called also Maison Dieu (16), the Star (17), the Moon or Luna (18), the Sun (19), the Last Judgment (20), the Universe (21), and the Foolish Man (0), or the zero card.

Some idea will be gained of the immense significance lying behind these cards of the major arcana if we give a brief note of one or two of them. Thus (1) is deemed to represent God, man, and the universe in the respective capacities of Creator, receiver, and transformer. It is the first card, and contains within itself the seed or potentiality of the whole evolution of the remainder.

This first card represents the three mystic divisions of the Tarot major arcana into three septenaries, or sevens. The first of these, regarded again as a whole, will represent the creative principle, the second seven the receptive principle, and the third the transformer. These again are the Divine, human, and natural worlds.

Now, if we take the second card, the Pope or High Priestess, we see in this the foreshadowing of the receptive principle. For God, understood as the Father, reflects Himself, and gives birth to God the Son, who is His negative principle, by the force of His own power and might, inflicted upon pure passivity.

The third card, the Empress, shows the vivifying influence, or vitalising fluid, to complete the first trinity, of the Holy Ghost, as issuing from the other two. This first perfect trinity paves the way for the Emperor, the triumph of spirit over matter in the first Divine man, Adam-Eve, male and female, as the fourth card.

Regarded symbolically, this represents the transition from God made maifest to the other series which follow—the more human.

In this fourth card are reflected the capacities that have gone before. The Will, the Father; the power of emanation; and the vitalising creative fluid, the soul of the universe.

Thus this great series of cards is derived one from the other, and has analogies that run through the biological, astrological, metaphysical, emotional, logical, and astronomical worlds, as a key to evolutionary and esoteric science.

To complete the idea of evolution, of the immersion of the spiritual in the material world, we need only glance at the eighteenth card, Luna, or the Moon. This card depicts a meadow feebly lighted by the moon, which drips blood. A dog and a wolf are howling at the moon. A crayfish is climbing out of the water between the two animals. This records pictorially and symbolically the soul at its last gasp in the clutch of matter.

Now look at (19) the Sun. Here we see the ascendancy of spirit beginning to reassert itself. The sun sheds drops of gold upon two naked children in a walled enclosure. Evolution, as a descent, has reached and passed its culminating point, and begins its upward swing on the other side of the arc.

But our readers may say all this has little to do with fortune telling. Really it has everything to do with it, if it is borne in mind that the symbolism employed here is to get basic principles displayed so that they may, in combination, express, when afforded the opportunity, what is in store for the consultant, for we must remember that there is no such thing as chance.

It would not be possible to give here a complete guide to the Tarot card meanings, even if the whole of this book was devoted to it. But we can show that the Tarot is responsible for many of the meanings given to the ordinary cards.

A key to the first principles of the divining Tarot is as follows. Regard the ten cards of the suits—Sceptres, Cups, Swords, and Pentacles, or Money—as divided into three groups of three each, and then there is one card, the tenth (ten), left over. This last card is determined in value by those which follow it.

The three groups, of three each, are regarded as the commencement, opposition, and equilibrium. Set out in tabular form this will be recognised more easily.

CARD		
1 (Ace)	Commencement	of *Commencement*
2	Opposition	
3	Equilibrium	
4	Commencement	of *Opposition*
5	Opposition	
6	Equilibrium	
7	Commencement	of *Equilibrium*
8	Opposition	
9	Equilibrium	
10	Undetermined	

These three terms are again those really of the first three cards of the major arcana, of Thesis, Antithesis, Synthesis, of Creation, Reception, Reproduction, of Brahma, Siva, Vishnu. If we apply this key, we see that the Ace represents the initiation of an enterprise, the deuce records its opposition, the three the realisation of its beginning. The four is the real beginning of the opposition, five is the opposition to the obstacles, and six means the obstacles are now triumphant; seven means success of the enterprise, eight the opposition to its success—only partial success; nine, success is realised or continued.

If we now remember that Cups or Hearts mean preservation or love, that Swords or Spades means transformation, hatred, or war, that Sceptres or Clubs mean creation, enterprise, or agriculture, and that Pentacles or Money mean development, money, or trade, we can apply the master key pretty simply.